10 Best Parenting Ways to Ruin Your Child

Israel Galindo

10 Best Parenting Ways to Ruin Your Child
© 2003, Israel Galindo.
All rights reserved.

Published by Educational Consultants
www.galindoconsultants.com

ISBN 0-9715765-0-5

Printed in the United States by:
Morris Publishing
3212 East Highway 30
Kearney, NE 68847
1-800-650-7888

CONTENTS

INTRODUCTION

This book is based on the popular seminar presentation "10 Best Parenting Ways to Ruin Your Child." Once, when the author presented this workshop in a church in Northern Virginia, he arrived to find that the host church had printed up flyers to announce the event. Picking up one of the flyers from a stack on a foyer table he noticed that someone had taken several flyers and crossed out "Ruin" and written, in what was obviously a child's handwriting "Love" in its place, thereby changing the title to "10 Best Parenting Ways to ~~Ruin~~ LOVE your Child."

That innovative child had set out to correct what was obviously a grievous error in her eyes. Of course, she didn't get the playfulness in the title. In reviewing these ten parenting errors what is intended is to help us find healthier ways to parent precisely because we love our children.

As you read through each of the 10 Best Ways, look for three main points: (1) the consequence of practicing the parental behavior in question; (2) the underlying rule to follow in the particular circumstance; and (3) the child's need associated with the particular parenting behavior.

In each of the 10 Best Ways we focus not on trying to "fix" our children, but on learning how to engage in better parenting behavior. The truth is that most of us learn our parenting skills in our family of origin, from our own parents, for better or for worse. Few of us learn our parenting skills in college (in fact, even if colleges attempted to teach parenting skills, few of us would effectively learn them in that context). Most parenting workshops seem to focus on changing the child's behavior instead of giving attention to the most important key to a child's health and well-being: on how well parents parent.

As you read through the 10 Best Ways, focus on changing yourself, rather than on changing your children. The extent to which we can be better parents is the extent to which our children will themselves become better parents—the family you provide for them is the only school for parenting they will ever attend.

Remember William Gibson's prayer in *A Mass for the Dead*, "What I pray for this year is not the remission of my sins, but the wit to remember them when they come back to me as my offspring's."

1. Put your child's happiness first as the guiding value in your home.

This "best parenting way to ruin your child" is listed first, because it is the most fundamental to understanding healthy and unhealthy ways to parenting. Let's face it, who among us doesn't want our children to be happy? Remember holding your child soon after he or she was born and having someone ask, "What do you most want for your child?" Most of us respond by saying, "I just want her to be happy."

There's nothing wrong with wanting our children to be happy. But what we often fail to understand is that ensuring our child's happiness is not a fundamental parental responsibility. That's a hard one to accept, given our society's shared "myth of happiness" that springs from even our founding documents and the declaration that we have an inalienable right to "life, liberty, and the pursuit of happiness."

The reality is that happiness is a transitory emotional state. Happiness is fleeting, illusory, and more often than not dependent on any number of temporary states: the weather, our health, our attitude, our level of maturity, our worldview, our level of egocentricity. The bottom line is that we are not responsible for, nor do we have the power to ensure our children's happiness.

There's a great theological truth behind this. Despite what you may have been told, *God is more interested in your relationship with him than he is with your happiness.* That does not mean that God does not care about you. It just means that your happiness is not the guiding principle out of which God operates in his relationship with you.

To illustrate this, let's look at that central focal point of our faith that defines much of our Christian belief, the Cross. When Jesus was hanging on the cross, at the horrendous culmination of his ministry and manifest destiny, what do you imagine was God's question to his son at that moment? Was God's question, "Son, are you happy?" Of course not, that would be cruel.

God's question for Jesus at the moment he was hanging on the cross was, "Son, do you still love me? At this moment, despite it all, despite the circumstance, despite the pain, do you still love me?" God defines his relationship with us not on transitory and circumstantial feelings of happiness, but on the binding commitment of mutual love. God is more concerned with your relationship with him than he is with your happiness.

I am amazed that children understand this intuitively. Has your child ever accidentally broken something expensive or valuable in your home? Do you remember his or her reaction? Your child's body goes stiff, he gets that terrified look in his face that indicates he knows he's done something terrible, and then he asks this question: "Mommy, are you mad at me?" You know that what he's really asking is, "Mommy, do you still love me?" Your child wants to know if, despite the circumstance, his relationship with you is defined by the circumstance or by love?

The consequence of living out of the principle of putting your child's happiness first as the guiding principle in your home is that you will give your child a skewed view of reality. Your children will soon come to believe that others are in the world to provide for their happiness, a false belief that can bring tragic results.

Children need parents who are centered and mature enough to make decisions based on what is best for their children, not necessarily on what will make their children happy. For some years I was a principal at a private elementary school. One day, on the first day of school, not twenty minutes after the first bell of the day, my secretary knocked on my door and said, "There's a parent here to see you."

A young mother, new to the school, entered the office, sat down, and said, "I want to take my daughter out of school."

"My stars," I thought to myself, "What could we have done that would cause a parent to want to take her child out of school twenty minutes into a new year?!"

"Can you tell me why?" I asked her.

She looked at me rather sheepishly and said, "My daughter doesn't like it here."

Something in the way she said that, along with the guilty look on her face, told me she knew exactly what was going on. But I also perceived that I wasn't going to win this one, so I decided to salvage the situation at some level.

"Why did you choose this school?" I asked.

"Because it's supposed to be a very good school," she replied, a bit puzzled at the question.

"Let me get this straight," I said, "You chose this school because you want your daughter to have a good education?"

"Yes," she replied.

"And you paid for the first month's and last month's tuition?"

"Yes," she replied.

"And you paid for her books, and bought her school uniform?" I pressed.

"Yes," she replied, slumping into her seat.

"And despite the fact that you believe this is a good school you're going to take your daughter out of class the first day of school because she doesn't *like* it?" I asked.

She gave me a helpless look, saying, "She doesn't like it here."

I thought to myself, "I don't want to be around to witness what this kid's going to be like when she's a teenager!" Here was a mother who had such little tolerance for her daughter's momentary unhappiness (few children are thrilled at their first day at *any* school) that she was willing to sacrifice the lifelong benefits of a good foundational education for her child's momentary happiness. This was a parent who failed to live up to her obligation to do what was best for her child because she had a skewed understanding of the parental relationship. She placed her concern for her child's happiness over her responsibility to act lovingly.

The first best parenting way to ruin a child is to make trying to make him or her happy the central value in your home.

2. Make your child the focus of your marital relationship.

I'm always amused watching two people who meet for the first time. After an initial pleasant greeting, there's the exchange of names, perhaps some indication of mutual connections ("I'm Stephen's dad," or "I'm Sarah's mom," or "I'm a friend of Paul, I was the best man at his wedding.") and then there is an awkward silence inevitably followed by a discussion on . . . the weather.

"Sure has been hot lately," one says.

"Yes, it sure has," the other replies, "and the humidity doesn't help."

"Oh the humidity is awful," continues the one.

"They say it'll cool down by next week."

"Really? That's good. We could use some rain, though," challenges the first person.

"Yes, it's been so dry. My lawn is almost brown!"

These meteorological discussions can go on for some time. On several such occasions I myself have eventually gotten to share my well-rehearsed story of surviving hurricane Andrew, my personal ultimate weather-related story. The next time you meet a stranger, see how long it takes before you both start talking about the weather. The reason this happens is that dual relationships are difficult to maintain. The basic relational unit is the triangle. This is because a triangulated relationship handles anxiety more efficiently.

Even in families without children, the familial relationship of the couple is triangulated. The couple will elect a family pet, an in-law, money, careers or jobs, or some other issue to form the third corner of the triangle. But when children come along, they become the natural and convenient point of the triangle that defines the family relationship. When a family becomes child-focused, the child often takes on the parental anxiety that his or her parents do not handle well.

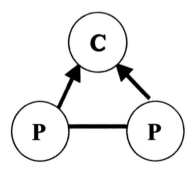

A child-focused family

The consequence of making your child the focus of your marital relationship is that you will erode the primary relationship in the family: the adult relationship between the parents.

We're not suggesting that you ignore or neglect your children. As loving parents, that won't happen. You'll care for and provide well for your children. But because children take so much personal energy, time and attention, it is not difficult to one day discover that somewhere along the way your marital relationship has shifted from focusing on the marriage to focusing on the children. This is detrimental to both your marriage and to your children. The fact is that to the extent that you invest in fostering a mature marital relationship, is the extent to which your children will most benefit from you as parents.

Simply put, the only place your child will learn what it means to be a mature adult is from watching and living with mature parents. The only place your child will learn how to be a good marriage partner and how to be a good parent is from you. He or she will not learn that in school, nor from a college course, nor from a workshop. A boy will learn about how to treat women from his father. He will learn to respect women to the extent that he observes his father treat his mother with love and respect. And paradoxically, a girl will learn what it means to be a women from her father. Not in the sense of how to be feminine, but in the sense of her worth as a person. As she observes how her father treats her mother, she learns whether a woman is an equal partner in the marriage relationship, or a convenient maidservant. And she will carry that learned concept of her own personhood into her own relationships.

The rule is that parents must resist making their marriage child-focused. Each partner must commit to maintaining a marriage-focused relationship. Remember that dual relationships are difficult to maintain, so it's not that each partner invests in the other *person*, rather, each invests in the *marriage*. Investing in a marriage-focused marital relationship is the best gift parents can give their children.

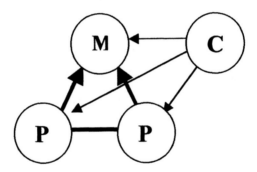

A marriage-focused family

The fact of the matter is that your job of parenting is over by the time your child is six years old (depending on how old your child is when you're reading this, that may be good news or bad news). In other words, whatever those things are that our children need from us as parents, they must get them from us by the time they reach six years of age.

By the time children reach six years of age, they:

- Are half as tall as they will be their entire life
- Have learned half of what they will have learned their entire life
- Acquired language and most of their life vocabulary
- Developed their basic sense of Self, including basic values, world view, and faith orientation
- Acquired and incorporated their family role
- Developed their basic sense of self-esteem
- Developed their basic gender orientation
- Developed their basic prejudices
- Developed their basic conscience.

Those things our children need from us that only we can give then as parents, must be realized before they reach the age of six. After that our job of parenting is over. Legally, we are required to feed and clothe them until they are self-sufficient and are of legal age (those two items not being necessarily the same), but our job of parenting is over pretty quickly. After age six we should just enjoy the gift from God that our children truly are, but our job of *parenting* is over.

This helps put things in perspective. While our job as parents is over in a brief six years, when we took our marriage vow it was for a lifetime's relationship ("till death do us part.").

You married your spouse for a lifetime; you'll be a parent only six years. Maintaining a marriage-focused marital relationship will help ensure that family priorities are balanced. A child-centered marriage is to the detriment of each member of the family.

3. Do things for your child that she can do for herself.

O ne of the most important truths about being a parent is that from the first day your child arrives home it is your job to help him or her leave. The test of successful parenting is how well we as parents have been able to prepare our children to be independent, self-sufficient adults. One long suffering parent said, "You know you've succeeded as a parent, not when your kids leave home, but when they're able to afford their own health insurance!"

The third best parenting way to ruin your children is for you to do things for them that they can do for themselves. The consequence of this parenting behavior is that it will rob your child of his or her ability to be independent. Eventually you will create either an underfunctioning child or an overfunctioning child.

The rule is that the more you do for your child the more dependent he or she will become. The only way to nurture responsible, independent children is to give them responsibility and then hold them accountable. This applies even to preschool-aged children. A preschooler may not be able to hang his or her clothes up in the closet, but he or she can pick them up from the floor and place them on the bed or in a hamper. Even a preschooler can learn to pick up his or her toys from the living room and take them to the bedroom or den.

Perhaps the question a parent needs to ask is, "How long do I want to be parenting my offspring?" I am perpetually amazed at the things I see middle-aged adults do for their adult children: pay the car insurance, cover a missed rent payment for an apartment, pay for car repairs, help their grownup child move from one apartment or house to another. One adult parent I know was still buying her 25-year-old daughter underwear!

These overfunctioning/underfunctioning relationships don't happen overnight. They are the result of years of patterned family behavior. One year when I was an elementary school principle a fourth-grader that had been in our school since his preschool years was getting into trouble. He wasn't turning in his homework or school projects. Because his grades were starting to slip we called a parent conference to see how we as a school could be of help.

During the course of our meeting with the parents we came to find out that the mother had been doing his homework all these years (something his teachers suspected on occasion). Now that her son was in fourth grade and the math was getting harder, mom had tried to put her foot down about the homework. But by that time the pattern had been set, the boy didn't have the necessary attitude, patience, or discipline to do his own homework. He had learned that if he waited long enough, mom would do the homework or science project rather than have her son get a failing grade. Ironically, rather than helping, she was setting him up for a more severe failure in life.

As our parent-teacher meeting continued, we discovered that not only was mom doing the fourth-grader's homework, but she was still giving him his nightly bath! The family pattern of an overfunctioning parent and an underfunctioning child carried well beyond schoolwork, to the extent that this young man didn't even bathe himself without his mother's help.

On discovering the extent of the child's lack of independence we called a "time out." We told the family not to worry about the academics for the moment, that we had some deeper issues to worry about. We recommended a therapist for the family to see, which they did. Eventually, both mother and son were able to re-work their parent-child relationship on a healthier level.

Children need to learn competence and mastery over their world and self. As soon as possible, they need to learn to take responsibility for themselves. Effective parents work at helping their children gain independence and competence. Again, how long do you want to be parenting your child?

I remember one of those gratifying parenting moments when one realizes that, "Hey, we must be doing something right with these kids." One day our youngest son, then twelve years old, came to me and said, "Dad, I want a color TV for my room, will you buy it for me?"

"I'm not going to buy you a color TV," I replied. "But if you earn the money for it, I'll *let* you have a color TV in your room." Since we had a rule in our home that the kids could not watch TV on school days and only three hours on the weekend, I thought that it probably wouldn't do much harm for him to have a TV in his room. Besides, I thought to myself, where was he going to get the $300 to buy a color TV?

Two weeks later, my son shows me a flyer from an electronics store, points to a color TV and says, "Dad, drive me to the store, I want to get this one."

"You got the money?" I asked, expecting an argument about how I should spring for it with my hard earned money.

"Yes," he said proudly, "I even have enough for the tax!" And with that he pulled out a wad of cash to prove it.

For two weekends he'd called a group of his friends together and went door-to-door in our neighborhood convincing people to let him wash their cars for them. In two weeks he had enough to buy his TV.

Needless to say I was impressed, and relieved. "Whew," I thought to myself, "I'm not going to have to worry about this one. He's going to do well in this world." He'd learned that his parents will provide for his *needs*, but they weren't necessarily going to provide for everything he *wants* (an important difference some adults don't seem to be able to understand). And he learned that he did not have to be dependent on his parents for things he wants. He was goal-directed, took responsibility for himself, figured out a way to raise money, and provided for himself. There's a lot to say for a kid who has learned those lessons at twelve years of age! But I know too that he would not have learned them if he had had parents that provided for every luxury he wanted.

Children don't need "things" from their parents. But they need desperately those intangibles that only parents can provide: values, character, challenge, habits, direction, example, discipline, and guidance.

4. Map out your child's life based on your own dreams and aspirations.

In the popular movie "Jerry McGuire," the film's title character falls in love with the female lead. In a very romantic scene the protagonist confesses his love to the girl by saying, "You complete me," a phrase made maddeningly memorable if only because of the endless play time the movie's theme song received on the radio.

That sentiment, "You complete me," makes for an emotionally romantic Hollywood movie moment, but it's a guarantee for a dysfunctional relationship!

The truth is that we weren't created to need another person to *complete* us. God just didn't create us that way. You are a whole and complete person in and of your individual self. But because intimate relationships involve sharing of ourselves, we often are blinded to that reality. I see the results of this most often when counseling recently divorced women. They have invested so much Self into their relationship with another person that they cannot fathom themselves as "complete" persons without another. They have given away a type of Self that cannot be shared.

In the same way, parents who cannot recognize where they end and their children begin as persons run the risk of doing great harm to their children. A parent that invests self-worth, deferred dreams, esteem, reputation, and personal hopes in their children rob them of their own destiny.

Mapping out your child's life based on your own dreams and aspirations robs your child of the ability to discover his or her own destiny in life and of the opportunity to shape his or her own aspirations. There are two possible outcomes to this parenting behavior: you'll develop a self-less child who is not able to make a meaningful life without depending on another, or you will create a rebellious child who will reject others from sharing his or her life. Either way, you will create a bitter child.

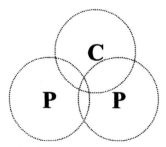

An enmeshed family group with two parents and a child with no sense of personal boundaries

The rule is that parents must learn to respect the personal boundaries of each family member. Your job as a parent is to rear a child who will have the capacity to be his or her own person.

Family relationships that lack clear personal boundaries are enmeshed. The individuals in those families have difficulty knowing their own minds, desires, and wills. When one person stubs their toe, the other says, "Ouch!" In those families no one is in charge and everybody is in charge. Family members do not know who they are apart from the others.

Persons with unclear personal boundaries often lack a strong core or "Real Self." The Real Self is that part of ourselves that we do not share with others. It is the "real you" and it needs no external support, is non-negotiable, and is neither given up nor taken in relationships.

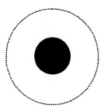

A person with a small Real Self gives away too much of Self

A person with a large Real Self maintains a strong integrity of Self

Our Pseudo Self, however, is that part of our makeup that we can and do share appropriately with others. The Pseudo Self has permeable boundaries, is influenced by circumstances, is negotiable when it experiences high anxiety or crises, is given and taken in relationships, and can become fused with other Pseudo Selfs. The more mature a person is, the bigger the Real Self and the smaller the Pseudo Self.

Children need to develop and become their own Selfs. This process begins early as the child learns to distinguish that he or she is separate from mother (at first the child does not realize that mother isn't just a feeding appendage). Later, the child learns that he or she is a separate individual apart from family, usually when they begin formal daycare or schooling experiences. But parents can interrupt that process when they try to live through their children's participation in sports or achievements in the arts or other activities. When parents try to "will" their children to value what they value, when they attempt to choose for their children's lives what they want for them (careers, mates, avocations), then parents deny their children of the most valuable thing they alone can provide: the gift to their children of their own lives and destinies.

Most parents don't do this intentionally. For example, it's no secret that the first-born child often takes on a lot of parental anxiety. Parents, and the extended family, invest a lot of emotional coin in that first child. Sometimes called the "Standard-bearer," the firstborn child is expected to carry on the family name (sometimes literally if a "Jr." or "II" is attached to the name), take over the family business, or to carry on the family traditions. It's no surprise then that firstborn children are some of the most conservative and tradition-minded persons around.

Paradoxically, the firstborn child often is told that "you can do anything you want in this world. You can accomplish anything you set your mind to." In reality, this is rarely true of firstborns—they know what's expected of them. Firstborns will tend to follow predictable life trajectories, they tend to be "good" children, do well in school (because they tend to relate well to adults), go to college, marry young, have a family, choose a career early, and provide mature leadership.

It is the second-born or youngest child in the family who can truthfully be told, "You can do anything you want; you can accomplish anything you set your mind to." Youngest children are the pioneers and explorers of the world (almost every famous explorer was a youngest, like Christopher Columbus). They buck convention, think easily outside the box, and are "different" enough to often feel like misfits in their own families. Often, they are the ones the family tries hardest to mold, "Why can't you be like your older brother?"

I see this in my own family. My oldest son is a straight-laced "A" student who made the Dean's List his first year in college (and maintains the most Spartan, neatest dorm room you've ever seen). He played sports and is leaning toward a career in criminal justice (a career that calls for no-nonsense adherence to law, fairness, and justice, respect for authority, and clear traditional moral boundaries). My youngest, on the other hand, loves jazz, is artistic, is a musician, and participates in an unconventional high school hi-tech academy program that uses innovative learning methods, creative group projects (like building robots), and which will give him a bucketful of college credits. Unlike his firstborn, classics-oriented dad, he wants to breeze through engineering school and get on with exploring what the world has in store for him.

It was my youngest son who, when he was thirteen years old, sauntered by the living room one day while I was preparing for a presentation on "Ten Best Parenting Ways to Destroy Your Child."

"What are you doing?" he asked, plopping down on the sofa.

"I'm preparing a workshop for parents," I relied.

He picked up the handout and gave me a suspicious look while he read down the list. When he got to number 4, "Map out your child's life based on your own dreams and aspirations," he cried out, "No! That's wrong! It's map out your child's life based on "*their*" dreams and aspirations! The child's, *not* the parents!"

It was all I could do to calm him down and explain that I was using a gimmick to communicate some important truths. I was, however, impressed that he "got it" so quickly. The tragedy is that children "get it" very quickly when parents try to shape their lives instead of giving the gift that is theirs: their own lives to live and shape. It is our calling as parents to rear our children with the capacity to be their own persons.

5. Get involved in fights between siblings.

The fifth best parenting way to ruin your children is to get involved in fights between siblings. And to make it worse, play the role of district attorney by questioning them as to who started the fight and taking sides. You know what this sounds like, don't you?

"Don't yell at your little sister!"

"Who started it?"

"Don't treat your younger brother that way, you're supposed to love your little brother!"

The consequence of this parenting behavior is that you interrupt and potentially destroy the development of your children's relationship with each other. The rule to follow for avoiding this disruptive parenting behavior is to raise your tolerance level for appropriate sibling conflict and stay out of their relationship.

I have a younger brother who, if you were to get to know me better, you may consider my "evil twin." We are very different, almost opposite. I'm an academic, he's a police officer. I'm short and stout, he's tall and thin. My idea of an ideal weekend is sitting on my Queen Anne easy chair reading the *New Yorker* and the *New York Review of Books*, his is to go out hunting. It goes on.

He and I do not have an adult sibling relationship to speak of. I have closer male friendships among professional colleagues than I do with my brother. When his first child was born, I mailed him a card that said, "Congratulations." No phone call, no visit. That gesture, one I would have extended to a church member of casual acquaintance, was as appropriate as our relationship allowed.

At one point I wondered how things came to be that way between us. I have distinct memories of our being good friends when we were young. I remember us playing together, sticking up for each other, and having fun together. So what happened between then and now in our relationship, I wondered.

I finally determined that when we were young children one of the values in our family was that we were a Christian family, and Christian families love each other and don't fight. Well, how do two boys relate to each other? They wrestle and roughhouse, play fight and make a lot of noise for starters. In a family sensitive to appear Christian, that kind of behavior was "fighting," and "Christian families don't fight."

So, every time my brother and I got "into it" (read: began relating to each other as boys are wont to do), our parents came between us. "Don't fight!" "Don't pick on your little brother." "You shouldn't talk to your brother that way." Inevitably, one or the other of us would wind up with the blame of who was at fault and received a more severe discipline than the other. This added only resentment to the episodes. Eventually, it seems, we stopped relating to each other to the point that our developing sibling relationship was aborted. The result was that as adults we have no sibling relationship to speak of.

Now with two boys of my own, you can imagine that I was determined that I was not going to do that to them. I worked hard at not getting in between their developing relationship as they grew up. Today they are good friends, to a great extent, I suspect, because I just stayed out of interfering with their relationship.

Things did not always go smoothly, or quietly, however. We're talking about two normal, healthy boys who stumbled along trying to work out their relationship. They fought, they argued, they were mean to each other, they tested and provoked each other . . . and tried their parents' patience to no end along the way.

But as parents we were committed to what we knew: siblings need to work out their own relationship—and it's got nothing to do with their parents. So we had to find ways to relate to each of them without relating, dictating to, or being willful about their relationship to each other. In other words, we had to work hard at not being the third point of a relational triangle.

Relational triangles form when the anxiety level of a dual relationship gets too hard to handle. Dual relationships are difficult to maintain as it is, but when things get hectic or intense the triangulating forces come into full play [see Appendix B for the Laws of Emotional Triangles].

As parents we are still responsible for teaching and coaching our children, we can't just abdicate the parental role and let them have at each other till blood flows. The trick is engaging in the delicate job of parenting appropriately and non-anxiously so as to not do harm to our children's developing relationship. In our family we had two basic rules: (1) you do not hurt someone physically, and (2) no name calling, because calling someone a name is intentionally trying to hurt someone emotionally (and kids know that, that's exactly *why* they call each other names!). Other than that, they had to find ways to work out their own relationship.

When our boys were very young and they were just learning how to relate to each other, we wound up throwing out a few really nice toys. That usually happened when one or the other used a toy as a weapon and hurt his brother. Our parental response was first, to avoid commenting on how we thought they should act toward each other (we avoided being willful and trying to tell them how they should feel about each other). And second, we reinforced the guiding value of the family. So on several occasions I found myself taking the toy in question and saying, "Boys, I don't buy you guys toys for you to hurt each other. Your relationship is more important than this toy, and so since you can't seem to be able to handle it, I'm going to throw this toy away. People are more important than things."

No blaming, no inquisition as to who started it or who was at "fault" (c'mon, you know they *both* were, it "takes two to tango," as they say), and no lectures as to how they were supposed to relate to each other. But it didn't take more than about three or four favorite toys in the garbage bin for them to figure out a way to relate without clobbering each other with a toy.

Later, when they were older, I'd sometimes be in the study and I'd become aware of the rising excitable tone of their play together. They are those occasions every parent has come to recognize. You become aware of certain hints that tell you, "in about a minute something's going to fly across the room and something's going to break or someone's going to get hurt." So, some wise parental intervention is in order. But remember, you need to avoid blaming, interrogating, fault-finding, or interrupting their relating to each other.

What I devised for those times was to keep a stack of sheets with math problems on my desk. When the boys were making too much noise for me to do some work or they were about to cross that line this side of a looming disaster, I'd hand each of them a sheet of math problems and say, "Guys, take a break and do these problems. Bring them to me when you're done so I can check them."

No blaming, no yelling, no fault-finding, and no punishment. More importantly, no comment on my part about how they should relate to each other.

It took all of 10 minutes for them to complete the sheets of math problems and return them to me. By that time they were calmer and went back to playing together at a lower decibel level. (As they got older the math problems got harder, at one point including legal-sized sheets with long division! This technique seems to have paid off some unanticipated dividends—both boys wound up being really good at math!).

Learning to relate to people is a lifelong task, and that is true of siblings too. So as a parent we need to expect that our children will continue to work at discovering how to relate to each other. When my oldest reached his adolescence his relationship with his younger brother changed. Older adolescent brothers can be rather cruel and insensitive toward younger pre-adolescent siblings—this seems to be especially true with brothers. Older brother doesn't like "little brother" shadowing him—and lets him know it in no uncertain ways.

It was painful watching our older son being so egocentric and cruel toward his younger brother. And it was just as painful to see how younger brother felt hurt by being mistreated by someone he looked up to. The one thing younger brothers need most from their older siblings is approval—the very thing that older siblings are loath to give to those below them.

The situation with my boys at that stage of their relationship got very painful to witness as a parent, and the temptation to intervene was great. However, to do so would make one the victim and the other the "bad" one. To perpetually rescue a child places him or her in the victim role. It sends the message that she is powerless to help herself and must be rescued.

Finally, primarily to lower my own anxiety and to live up to my responsibility as parent, I decided to take some kind of action. I went to my oldest son first. Rather than tell him how I thought he should treat his younger sibling (that would be willful) or tell him how disappointed his behavior was, I told him a story.

"Son, you know I have a younger brother," I said. And then I told him the story of the estranged relationship between my brother and me. I finished by telling him, "I hope you don't lose a friend in your younger brother. But that's going to be up to you."

Then I went to talk to my youngest son. I needed to avoid telling him how to relate to his older brother during that awkward stage of their lives and also avoid making him the victim. So to him I said, "Son, you know your brother is giving you a great gift these days."

"Huh?" he responded.

"Yes, it's true. You see, in your life you will run into a lot of jerks in the course of school and work. Your brother is giving you the opportunity to learn how to deal with the jerks of this world. Now I wish I could tell you how to handle them, but people have to figure that out for themselves. So, good luck with that. Knowing how creative and smart you are, I know it won't take you long to figure out how to handle your brother when he acts like a jerk."

That was the extent of my parental intervention. It was not easy to follow those basic relational rules: monitor your own anxiety, be non-reactive in your responses, do not be willful when dealing with your children by trying to impose your values or desires, and never get in a triangulated relationship by trying to change how two other people relate to each other. And, the most important one: trust your children to be able to find their own way.

We had to wait a while to see evidence that this parenting approach worked. But it was worth the wait and well worth avoiding the temptation to give in and intervene at times.

A couple of years ago our family was eating dinner at home. Both boys were in their teens then, and conversation around the table was lively. I wasn't paying too close attention to what happened next, but at one point our youngest spoke in a tone that made us all sit up and take notice.

He turned to his older brother and said forcefully and firmly but without yelling, "Doug, I was talking. You interrupted me and ignored me. That was rude and I don't appreciate it!"

Wow! How many adults do you know who can do that? At a moment of being upset he was non-reactive but a non-victim. He took responsibility for his feelings and held another person accountable for his actions. He had learned to handle himself with someone who was acting like a jerk, and learned very well at that!

Wise parents learn to increase their tolerance level for appropriate sibling conflict and to stay out of their children's developing relationships with each other.

6. Argue with your child.

When it comes to the parent-child relationship, I can think of no uglier scene than when a parent and child engage in a public display of a battle of wills. A parent will tell the child to do something and the child will argue back. Then the parent tries to reason with the child, and the child still refuses to obey. Then the parent resorts to threats, but the child continues to argue with the parent having learned from experience that parental threats are empty. The scary part is that the child's behavior indicates that she knows a terrible secret: the child has learned that if she continues to argue and embarrass the parent, she will eventually get her way. At the moment of engaging in that battle of wills, the parent has abdicated his or her parental role.

The consequence of this parenting behavior is that you elevate your child to the status of Parent and teach him that he has the right to question your judgment and decisions every time, in all things.

The rule is that you are the parent, and as such, you have more rights than your child. You also have the obligation to make certain decisions for your child, that's your job.

Despite appearances to the contrary, children need and want to know who the parent is in the family. They intuitively know that their parents are supposed to be in charge and find security and order when parents maintain their responsible family role. While they may on occasion seem to be challenging parental authority, what is usually happening is that they are testing the stability of their world by pushing against the edges. Their desperate need is not to win, but to confirm what they need to know: that they can count on their parents to be parents.

Children are adept at discerning what the rules are. They learn quickly that they can get away with certain things at home that they cannot get away with at school, for instance. Or, they quickly pick up that they can behave a certain way at home with mom, but they'd better not even try that at the grandparents' home when visiting or staying over. I was always somewhat amused at parents who would observe their child's interaction with his or her teacher and other adults at school and remark, "How do you get him to do that?! I can't get him to do anything at home!" Obviously, the problem wasn't so much with the child as with the adults at home. His parents had trained him one way, the adults at school another, and the child was discerning enough to know the difference.

I remember, during a youth group outing of our church, giving a particular young man some specific instructions for something that needed to be done. He had a reputation of being a "difficult" youth, and watching his interaction with his parents made that apparent. As soon as I finished giving him instructions he began telling me why he couldn't or wouldn't do it. It was an automatic response on his part and he just kept on talking and talking. Finally, I looked him in the eye and said, "Herman, are you arguing with me?"

The response was dramatic. His eyes widened and his jaw hung open as it dawned on him what it was he was doing. Then he looked at me and said, "Oh," and immediately went and did what he was asked.

Younger children should not be allowed to argue with a parent, nor to question the reason why they are being told to do something. The parent may, however, choose to tell the child why they are being told to do something, and this is helpful because it teaches the child the value behind the action. So, a parent may say, "Mary, please pick up your toys from the living room now. We have company coming and we want the house to look nice." Or, "Billy, please give the dog a bath now, he's probably feeling uncomfortable and he's unpleasant to be around right now."

When your children become teenagers it becomes more important to share the reasons why they are being told to do something, and it becomes appropriate to negotiate on some things. If you tell your teenager to wash the car and he responds, "But I was going to go out with my friends this afternoon," it's o.k. to negotiate. You may respond by saying, "Oh, I didn't know. Thanks for telling me. But I need the car washed by Saturday afternoon."

That kind of response tells your child that you respect his interests, but that you still expect him to do what he's asked.

As with all of the parenting ways presented in this book, the hardest part will be to train yourself to respond differently. It helps, therefore to think ahead and anticipate what your healthy, non-reactive parental response will be when your child misbehaves or acts out. When our boys were younger, my wife and I had a set of cue phrases or words to help us respond non-reactively to the children. These helped the boys by getting them re-focused in times of anxiety or excitability.

For example on occasion we would visit the grandparents after church. On the way we'd pass any number of McDonald's restaurants (there seemed to be one on every block). When the boys would see one they'd yell, "Let's stop at McDonalds! We're hungry! I want a happy meal!" and so on ad nausea in an attempt to get mom and dad to pull over. If they continued after the first "No" response from either of us, we'd use a cue phrase that kept us from losing our tempers and helped them re-gain a right perspective on the world. That phrase was, "What you want is not important right now." This was not delivered with a mean spirit. It was just a statement of fact. If our family was on its way to visit the grandparents after church, then what they "wanted" at the moment was not at the center of the universe. And they understood that. They were able to center themselves and realize that "Oh, I remember now, I'm the child in the family and mom and dad are the parents. What I want isn't always the most important thing, and this is one of those times."

Children need their parents to be parents.

7. Allow your child to see that he or she makes you feel guilty.

Every time I think about dropping this "best parenting way to destroy your child" from the list, I come across clear evidence that I need to keep it in.

You know what this one sounds like, don't you?

"You never let me have any fun!"

"You don't love me!"

"But Billy's mom lets him! I wish I had a different family!"

"You don't care!"

"I hate you!"

Kids really know which button to push, don't they? They know exactly what to say to try to make us feel guilty. That's why they say those things! But one of the most detrimental parenting behaviors is to allow children to see that they can make you feel guilty.

The consequence of engaging in this parent behavior is that you teach your child that you are an emotional puppet that can be manipulated and used. After this pattern is set in your home, a child learns to relate to other persons the same way—"people are to be used to get my way or to comply with my desires."

The rule is to realize that no child can make you feel anything. No person can make you feel guilt, love, joy, fear, or any other emotion. These things come from within you, and you are the only one who is responsible for those feelings. Also, you are the only one who can choose to (or choose not to) feel a particular emotion, or to respond in a certain way regardless of how you feel at the moment. Note that we're not saying that you shouldn't *feel* guilty because of what your child says or does. If your response to the pointed words of a child is to feel guilty, that's an issue you need to work on. What we are saying is that *you shouldn't let your child <u>see</u> that he or she can make you feel guilty.* That's a power no child should be burdened with.

When I served as pastor of a local church, I remember a young lady coming to see me for some help. She was having trouble at home (you guessed it, "parent trouble"). At one point in the session I made some "helping comments" to her, reframing an understanding of her behavior toward her parents. She responded to these pointed statements on my part by saying (whining, really), "How can you say that? You hurt my feelings."

My response was to tell her, "I'm sorry, I'm not responsible for your feelings. My statements weren't intended to hurt you, and I have no power to make you feel one way or another."

From the blank look on her face it was apparent that no one had ever pointed this out to her before. But the conversation took off in a more honest direction from that point on. She was used to having people cave in to her by "taking care" of her feelings. When she was challenged to engage in a more honest dialogue, she was forced to respond on a more mature level.

The truth is that if you are a good parent, on occasion you will have to do things for and to your child that he or she will not like. Parenting involves taking responsibility in making some choices for your child that will not make them happy. Remember that theological truth: *God is more interested in your relationship with him than he is with your happiness*. The corollary is that you should be more interested in maintaining a healthy parent-child relationship with your children than you are with their momentary happiness.

Happiness is a transitory feeling, and what is best for us does not always make us happy. We do not need to feel guilty for doing what is best for our children even if they don't like it.

Children need to accept direction and nurture from the persons who know them best and are responsible for making decisions for them. And children need to learn to respect parents, not manipulate them as means to their ends. Remember that axiom: "Use things, love people." Children who see and learn that they can make their parents feel guilty are in danger of learning the wrong lesson: "Use people, love things."

8. Call on your spouse to be the disciplinarian.

Disciplining children is probably one of the least liked aspects of parenting. A good parent never actually *wants* to inflict discomfort on the child he or she loves. When a parent has to discipline a child, no one is happy.

However, providing discipline for our children, and meting out punishment, is an inescapable parental function. Unless your child is perfect (and therefore probably a bit creepy), you'll need to discipline your child at one point or another.

The eighth best parenting way to ruin your child, however, is to call on your spouse to be the disciplinarian in the family. This parenting behavior has the added bonus of not only being bad for your child, but bad for your marriage too.

You know what this one sounds like: "You just wait till your father gets home!" Or, "Just wait till your mother gets home, you'll be in big trouble then!"

The consequence of regularly practicing this parental behavior is that you teach your child that you (the parent) do not have the authority or the power to discipline him. Once again, this kind of behavior is an abdication of the parental role, one that leaves the child lost and looking for the "center" of his family life. Children's misbehavior often increases when parents abdicate their parental roles because they are trying to bring the world back into order by forcing the parent to assert herself. Children need to know who's in charge. They crave a secure moral center to their world.

The rule to follow is that whichever parent is present at the time of the infraction or misbehavior is the one who must administer the discipline. That discipline can be deferred if you are so flabbergasted by what your child has done. You may, for instance, say, "What you did was wrong, and right now, I'm not sure what your punishment should be. When your [father/mother] gets home, we'll talk about this and decide what your punishment will be." (This has the added advantage of having the kid sweat it out for a few hours wondering what will happen to him!)

One of the common mistakes that parents make in the area of discipline is not getting their act together ahead of time. Parents need to present a united front in matters of values and discipline. That means that investing some time discussing your family values and expectations is important. Decide together ahead of time what you both agree to be appropriate disciplines for specific infractions.

And of course, never undermine your spouse's authority in front of the children. If you disagree with an impromptu discipline meted out by your spouse, talk about it together later when you can do so in private. Avoid at all costs openly disagreeing about a child's discipline in the heat of the moment.

9. Tell your child to do something two or three times so he or she will know that it is not important to listen to you or follow directions.

If there is one rule that merits being titled "The Most Popular Top 10 Rule Used to Ruin Your Child," it's probably this one. I'm convinced that parents can save themselves (and their children) years of frustration by learning to avoid practicing this one.

I was sitting at the doctor's office a few weeks ago and witnessed one of the most blatant displays of this ninth parenting way to destroy a child. A mother and her small boy, he about seven years old, caught the attention of everyone in the crowded waiting room with the scene they were making. The mother had told the boy to sit down, something he apparently was not willing to do. For the next four minutes (yes, I counted) the mother repeated the command over and over. Then she resorted to threats, which escalated to her pulling on his arm, and finally to total exasperation at which time the mother dragged the child out of the waiting room and into the hallway out of sight, but not out of the hearing of the spectators. We heard mother's muffled screech followed by a solid smack. Shortly afterwards mother and child returned to the waiting room, she much embarrassed and flustered, he teary and pouting.

The consequence of practicing this ninth parenting behavior is that you will train your child that he or she doesn't have to listen to you the first time you say something. Your child learns that whatever you say can be ignored. Often the result of this parenting behavior comes to fruition when the child enters school or another formal instructional setting. Children who grow up with parents who repeat directions often have difficulty adjusting to a setting where other adults expect to be heard and obeyed immediately when instructions are given.

At the school where I served as principal we had a school-wide discipline program. The teachers could decide on whatever rules worked best for their individual classroom, and so each teacher had a list of no more than seven rules posted in their classroom (no more than five rules for the younger elementary classes). But *every* classroom had to have the following rule listed *first*: "Follow directions the first time they are given." The teachers and staff spent the entire first week of school intentionally training (and sometimes re-training) students to obey that first universal rule. Once we had that down we knew that we were able to avoid untold numbers of incidents and behavior problems during the school year.

With 800 kids interacting together on any given day, maintaining order and discipline was critical to being able to provide a good learning environment. Can you imagine what it would be like if every teacher had to repeat every direction, instruction, or command three or four times? Can you imagine the chaos if every student knew that they could ignore instructions the first time they were given?

The fact of the matter is that, as psychologist Marvin Silverman says, there is no child living on this planet that cannot follow directions the first time they are given (barring neurological or hearing problems).

The rule is, you tell your child the direction or instructions *once*, then follow up with a consequence if there is no appropriate response. It's as simple as that. However, if you are in the habit of telling your child to do something two or three times before he or she actually obeys, your hardest job is going to be to re-train yourself. You've already trained your child *not to listen* to you. You'll have to train yourself first before you can begin to re-train your child.

If you repeat directions two or three times and then yell at your child when you lose your temper at being ignored, you wind up rewarding your child with an emotional release. Most kids will take any attention from a parent they can get (sadly, for many children, abusive attention is preferable to being ignored) and besides, watching mom or dad lose their cool is fun. As an added consequence, you model for your child how to handle disappointments and setbacks: throw a tantrum! Avoid raising your voice and displaying anger toward your children when they disobey.

One mistake parents make when trying to put into practice this approach to giving directions is that they go overboard on the consequences they choose. Keep in mind that a consequence does not have to be a painful punishment or a "big deal." For children, a consequence just has to be a major inconvenience. You want to inconvenience your child, not yourself!

If you tell your child to set the table for dinner, for example, and he doesn't immediately do it, you don't come back ten minutes later and say, "Tim, I told you to set the table, now please go do it." Timmy has no real reason to believe that you actually want the table set. After all, you waited ten minutes to repeat the instructions and you'll probably wait ten more minutes and repeat it again as far as he's concerned.

What a parent needs to do is tell Timmy to set the table, and if Timmy does not do so, then the parent needs to say to Timmy, "Tim, I told you to set the table and you didn't. You know we expect you to do what you're told right away.

Because you did not obey you'll loose ten minutes of TV time today."

The parent then makes sure that Timmy sets the table. Taking TV away for the whole day really is not a punishment. Timmy will find something else to do and the punishment will not be an inconvenience in any way. But later that day, as Timmy watches his favorite program, the parent waits till ten minutes before the show is over and says, "Timmy, today you didn't set the table when you were told and the consequence was losing ten minutes of TV time. Please turn off the TV now." You can be sure Timmy's response will be, "Aw, mom!"

Sending kids to their rooms is hardly an inconvenient consequence in most homes. Our kids had TV, Nintendo, toys, books, stereos, you name it. It was a treat being sent to their rooms. So, on occasion, when both were guilty of an infraction or of not following directions the first time they were given, we'd send them to *each other's room!* They really hated that! Keep the pain where it belongs, don't inconvenience yourself while trying to discipline your child.

Children need a structured world in which they know their place, who people are and what to expect of them, and they need to know that their parents are in charge. They need to know that they can trust and have confidence in their parents.

10. Drop your child off at church and then go have breakfast or cut the grass or play a round of golf and then pick them up after church.

One frightening unspoken realization we all live with as parents is the truth that our children learn more from what they observe of us than from what we tell them. The old axiom, "Do as I say, not as I do," is not an operational dynamic when it comes to parenting.

Faith is the single most critical human dynamic that we possess. It is formed in the first six months of life and it is the last and only personal resource we will have during our last six months of life. A child whose faith suffers setbacks in his or her development during the first six months to one year of life will live trying to overcome that deficit for the rest of his or her life. And at the last stage in life, the extent to which one has a fully realized faith will prove to be the extent of the most important personal resource available for making a "good death." At the end of life, little else matters—not the amount of liquidity in your portfolio, not your faded golf skills, not your past professional accomplishments, not your collection of china, antiques, or coins. All those material things, along with all the illusions we surround ourselves throughout life, fade away and leave us with the only real personal resource that gives life meaning: our personal faith.

The consequence of engaging in the parenting behavior of dropping your child off at church and skipping out on yourself attending and participating is that you will teach your child that faith, and participating in a faith community, is not important. At the very least it will send a double message to your child, and he or she will learn not to believe you when you say certain things (hypocrisy is a concept learned early by children).

Perhaps the most tragic consequence of engaging in this tenth best parenting way to destroy your child is that you will rob yourself of one of the greatest resources your family will ever have: a community of people who can share in supporting you in rearing your children. Often, in parenting workshops, I get asked the question from a single parent (usually a mother), "What about those of us who don't have a spouse?"

My response is to point out the importance of choosing healthy communities of which to be a part of and in which to participate. Even as a parent with a partner spouse, I was intentional about the role that my faith community played in the lives of my sons. I would intentionally point out (and I mean that literally) other adults in our congregation and say to my sons, "See that person? That's a decent man." Or, "See that women? That's a great Christian person."

We don't rear our children in a vacuum. If the tragic incidents at places like Columbine have taught us anything, it is this: we all have a real stake in how other people rear their children. Consider: somebody else's son will marry your daughter, somebody else's daughter will marry your son. Don't you hope that that person has done a good job of parenting? Don't you pray that that person has done a good job of rearing a mature, emotionally healthy, decent person? This is what communities help each other to do.

The rule is, first, find a healthy community of faith, and then participate fully in the life of the people of that community. We've said that faith is the single most critical human dynamic. In our society, there are only two institutions exclusively dedicated to fostering the faith of children: the family, and the church.

A child who has been gifted with a family and a church dedicated to nurturing his or her faith is doubly blessed.

11. Eight Worst Parenting Things to Say to a Preschooler

1. **Don't Touch** (unless it's something you *want* your preschooler to discover). Preschoolers learn about themselves and their world through discovery, and the primary way they achieve that is through their senses. Preschoolers need to touch everything, and they're tempted to taste everything! Encourage your preschooler's natural tendency to make sense of his or her world through touch.

2. **Stop laughing.** The world will cause you child to stop laughing soon enough—don't you, as a parent, be the one to shrivel up the spontaneous spirit of joy your child possesses. A preschooler's laughter is unrestrained, loud, and sometimes inappropriate. Raise your tolerance level for noise for a few years, and don't let your embarrasment be the motivation for squelching your child's spirit of joy.

3. **Walk Faster; Keep Up.** Preschoolers live in their own frame of time. Most of the things that make us feel rushed are off their radar. Imposing our time schedule on preschoolers only frustrates them. The world will do too good a job of rushing your child through childhood. Give your child the gift of enjoying

childhood—you'll reap great benefits in allowing your child to teach you to slow down.

4. **Be quiet.** Say this too often to your preschooler and he or she just might. And by the time they're teenagers, you'll be asking, "Why don't you talk to me anymore?" Children feel valued when they learn that their parents care enough to listen to them.

5. **Be careful.** Preschoolers learn by experiences; allow yours to have them. Bumps and bruises will be a part of your preschooler's adventures in discovery. Resist giving in to the myth of "safety" that permeates our culture.

6. **Don't get dirty.** Children learn by doing, and dirt never hurt anyone. Don't be so squeemish about dirt that you rob your preschooler of engaging the world. Scrub them clean for Sunday church, but allow them the freedom to enjoy their world.

7. **Be good.** If by telling your preschooler "Be good," you mean, "Act grown up, like an adult," then it's better to keep your sentiment to yourself. Not only does your preschooler not have the ability to "act grownup," it's totally inappropriate. Preschoolers should act like preschoolers—allow your child to mature at his or her own pace.

8. **Why did you do that?** Preschoolers—and most adults for that matter—aren't self aware enough to know why they do certain things.

Asking your preschooler this question only serves to develop inappropriate guilt. Rather than interrogate your preschooler when he or she does something wrong, choose to make it a teaching moment.

Appendix A
Qualities of a Healthy Family

Can remain flexible in times of crises rather than become rigid

Affirms and supports each member as a distinct individual

Exhibits humor and creativity

Maintains and clarifies personal boundaries

Emphasizes the individual and family strengths over weaknesses

Works on solutions rather than blame

Encourages individual values, respect for personal choices and opinions

Develops a strong sense of trust among her members

Fosters a sense of shared responsibility for family issues

Teaches a clear sense of right and wrong

Celebrates and fosters rituals and traditions

Teaches and models appropriate altruism and service to others

Fosters a positive and practical religious faith

Shares in leisure time and interests

Respects boundaries of privacy among family members

Can make use of support systems when needed without becoming dependent on them

Can absorb outside anxiety and toxicity without threat to family individuals

Operates within the balance of respecting individual responsibilities and appropriate overfunctioning

Adapted from Dolores Curran, *Traits of a Healthy Family.* Used with permission.

Appendix B
Laws of Emotional Triangles

1. An emotional triangle consists of any three members of a relationship system or any two members of any relationship system and an issue or symptom

2. Emotional triangles form when anxiety becomes intolerable in a relationship and the partners "conspire" to reduce that anxiety by focusing on a third person, group or issue

3. Individuals are triangled when they become the focus of the unresolved issues of two others, or when they get caught in a position of being responsible for the relationship of two others, or another and his or her symptom or problem

4. Individuals who become triangled will have a harder time healing from whatever ails them, and they will find their thinking and functioning hindered

5. Paradoxically, efforts to change emotional triangles through the constant application of strong will generally produces the opposite intent, or at the very least will prove to be counterproductive

6. The stress and eventual burnout of leaders in a system (for example, parents in a

family) has less to do with hard work than with becoming emotionally triangled

7. The way out of the triangled position in an emotional triangle is to make the other two parts responsible for themselves and for their own relationship with the other.

Adapted from Edwin Friedman, *Generation to Generation.* Used with permission.

Appendix C

Birth Order Characteristics

Original challenges:

Only child	How to play alone without feeling lonely
First born	Loss of mother's love to the new baby
Second born	Being outdone by the first born
Third born	Being shamed by the second born
Fourth born	Being excluded by the third born

Strategies for solving the original challenges:

Only child	Create imaginary companions
First born	Wait for attention
Second born	Become perfectionistic
Third born	Be emotionally strong
Fourth born	Don't listen to self

Typical bad feeling:

Only child	Frustration
First born	Guilt
Second born	Inadequacy
Third born	Fear
Fourth born	Anger

Felt loss from childhood:

Only child	Freedom
First born	Love
Second born	Emotions
Third born	Protection
Fourth born	Belonging

Sense of justice:

Only child	Everything should be equal
First born	People should get what they deserve
Second born	What is necessary is just
Third born	There is no justice so you have to help the victims
Fourth born	There is no justice so you have to get even

Thought patterns:

Only child	Organize by tying up the loose ends
First born	Relate things to the future
Second born	Evaluate to discover flaws
Third born	Compare things to create new ideas
Fourth born	Analyze things from every angle

T-shirts:

Only child	Front: Leave me alone Back: I'd rather do it myself
First born	Front: I don't know Back: What do you think?
Second born	Front: That won't work Back: It's not good enough
Third born	Front: No problem Back: It doesn't bother me any
Fourth born	Front: Life isn't easy Back: You have to try hard

Type of emotional expression:

Only child	Demonstrative/sullen
First born	Agreeable/obnoxious
Second born	Friendly/critical
Third born	Sympathetic/aggressive
Fourth born	Empathy/anger

What causes anger:

Only child	Being intruded upon
First born	Shown lack of respect
Second born	Being criticized
Third born	Being putdown
Fourth born	Being blamed

Nature of humor:

Only child	Sarcasm - implying negative motives
First born	Shock - outrageous humor
Second born	Criticism - dry humor
Third born	Putdowns - embarrassing others
Fourth born	Insults - suggesting others are stupid/lazy/untrustworthy

Means of relating:

Only child	Projects own perceptions unto the other person imagining that the other person is the way he/she thinks they are
First born	Works to impress others to get their admiration
Second born	Offers constructive criticism to help others perform better
Third born	Looks for ways to help others so they will be pleased
Fourth born	Entertains others with witty expressions so they will want them around

Whom they understand on a gut level:

Only child	Just other only children
First born	Just other first borns
Second born	First and second borns
Third born	First, second and third borns
Fourth born	Everyone except onlies

Spirituality:

Only child	Ethical spirituality, wants to settle issues of right and wrong
First born	Relational spirituality, wants to have a loving community
Second born	Sacrificial spirituality, wants persons to commit themselves
Third born	Devotional spirituality, wants to gain strength through prayer
Fourth born	Mystical spirituality, wants to make contact with God

Relational problems:

Only child	Feels oppressed by others' negative feelings
First born	Feels obliged to satisfy others
Second born	Feels overwhelmed by others' anger
Third born	Feels obliged to help others
Fourth born	Feels trapped by others' feelings

The child within:

Only child	Feels smothered
First born	Feels abandoned
Second born	Feels neglected
Third born	Feels wounded
Fourth born	Feels isolated

Type of procrastination:

Only child	Puts off big jobs while doing small tasks
First born	Puts off doing practical things while dreaming of accomplishing great things
Second born	Puts tasks off till they can be done perfectly or till they have to be done
Third born	Puts tasks off for more interesting pursuits
Fourth born	Puts things off to spite others

Blind spot:

Only child	Inability to know what others think/feel
First born	Inability to tell what he/she thinks, feels, wants
Second born	Inability to know what others feel
Third born	Inability to cooperate
Fourth born	Inability to trust others

How they deal with boundaries:

Only child	Honors them for others and self
First born	Perceives others as having insurmountable boundaries
Second born	Strict boundaries defined by own rules
Third born	Cannot set boundaries to keep others out
Fourth born	Does not respect others' boundaries, has strict boundaries for him/herself

How each takes a walk in the woods:

Only child	Stays on the beaten path
First born	Plunges through the woods, gets into difficulty
Second born	Goes into the woods, watches the ground to avoid obstacles
Third born	Goes into the woods only to help someone else through the woods
Fourth born	Does not go into the woods, tells others where to go and how to get there

Strengths:

Only child	Organization, clarity of purpose, stable
First born	Visionary, leadership, compromise
Second born	Self-discipline, attention to detail, consistency
Third born	Compassion, imagination, practicality
Fourth born	Thinking, understanding, ambition

66

Parenting styles:

Only child	Allows children time and space
First born	Urges children toward dreams
Second born	Teaches self-discipline, obedience to rules
Third born	Protective on the one hand, challenging on the other
Fourth born	Is a companion to the children, inconsistent discipline

What passes for love:

Only child	Worry
First born	Agreement
Second born	Constructive criticism
Third born	Pleasing
Fourth born	Giving

Driving style:

Only child	Drives confidently expecting that everyone will drive correctly
First born	Drives cautiously as if others are out to get him/her
Second born	Drives angrily because others are violating the rules
Third born	Drives fearlessly or fearfully
Fourth born	Drives slowly while watching everything or aggressively in anger

Listening Style:

Only child	Puts own meaning into others' words
First born	Listens only to others, not self
Second born	Listens for mistakes
Third born	Interprets the motive for what is said
Fourth born	Listens only to self or the other, but not to both at the same time

Common phrases:

Only child	You know
First born	I don't know
Second born	You need to
Third born	No problem
Fourth born	Try hard

Interventions to get a hearing from:

Only child	I don't know about you but...
First born	You may not agree with this but...
Second born	This may not be perfect but...
Third born	This may be scary but...
Fourth born	This may be hard but...

Effective confrontations:

Only child	You can be angry if you want but...
First born	I would appreciate if you would...
Second born	Do you have any other criticisms?
Third born	I am disappointed...
Fourth born	Stop it!

Appendix D
Discipline Guidelines for Preschoolers

1. Set reasonable limits
2. Be consistent
3. Accept your child's feelings which he cannot control; but stop his disruptive and destructive behavior
4. Correct your child's behavior with love and respect
5. Avoid embarrassing a child
6. Don't force a child to say "I'm sorry."
7. Avoid threats
8. Notice and acknowledge your child's appropriate behavior
9. Don't force preschoolers to give up toys as a means of teaching about sharing
10. Provide a stimulating environment; in this way you reduce the posibility of behavior problems
11. Help your child feel good about himself.
12. Give emotional support to a child who misbehaves
13. Let your child learn from the natural or logical consequences of his or her actions
14. Give encouragement freely. It is inspiring.

Appendix E
Frequently Asked Questions

Q: I'm a single parent. Much of what you talked about seems to assume two parents. How does what you shared apply to single parents?

A: First, remember that the relational principles we identified apply to all parent-child relationships—even in terms of adult children and their parents. Second, let's realize that we don't rear our children in a vacuum. If the tragic, much-publicized school incidents of the past few years taught us anything, it is this: that we all have a great stake in how other people rear their children. Single parents should be more keenly aware than most of the importance of having a faith community as a primary resource. This is why participating in a healthy church community is important. Even as a parent with a spouse I was always very intentional about pointing out to my boys individuals in my church and saying, "See that person? That's a decent man." Or, "See that woman? That's a great Christian person."

As a single parent, you do not rear your children in a vacuum. And you don't have to rear your children alone. Take full advantage of what your faith community has to offer, both for you as a parent, and for your children.

Q: You said that we should never interfere in the relationship between siblings. But at some point you do need to interfere, we can't just let them beat on each other. How do you know when it's appropriate to intervene?

A.As I said, this is a tough one. I think the
answer lies in getting clear about the family
values and life principles that you will live by.
When you get clear about what those are, usually
it's not difficult to know when intervention is
appropriate. For example, in our family, the rules
were simple: (1) You don't physically hit anyone,
and (2) you don't call someone a name, because
that's just trying to hurt them emotionally. Since
those were the family rules, when siblings
violated those rules, intervention was appropriate.
But we worked at being sure they understood
that. So we'd say, "In our family we have two
rules . . . and since you broke the rules, there will
be a consequence." That kept the intervention
from being arbitrary, and kept us from blaming
one or the other.

Q.I'm a grandparent. When the kids visit in my
home I don't allow some of the things that
they seem to get away with at home. How do I
handle that?

A.Children have great capacity to be
discerning about what is expected of them.
It's very appropriate for you to let your children
(and their parents) know what you expect of them
by way of behavior in your home. Be sure to
enforce those rules—you can count on the kids
testing you to see if you really mean it. What is
not appropriate is for you to try to tell your
children how to parent their kids at home. Keep
the boundaries clear: you are the grandparent of
your children's children; you are not their parent.
Your children are your grandchildren's parents—

not you. Allow them to make their mistakes, you made your share of them.

Q: What about the issue of privacy and children's rooms? I've heard some people say that you should show absolute respect for your children's privacy and should never look around in their room. Is that appropriate?

A: This is a complex issue. One way to approach this is to consider what is appropriate for the developmental stage of your children. If they are preschool to school-aged, then their "right to privacy" probably is a moot issue. While it's their home too, you have greater responsibility as a parent for the home and for their well-being. Putting your young child's "right to privacy" above your parental responsibility is inappropriate.

Some rights are universal, some are earned. I think a child's "right to privacy" is earned. As your children become teenagers, their need for a sense of self-determination and privacy become important issues. But that doesn't trump the issue of trust in the parent-child relationship. I think one's right to privacy is contingent on the level of trust that exists in the relationship. If my child has proven that he or she cannot be trusted not to abuse the privacy I'm willing to give, then that breach of trust trumps any claims to a "right to privacy" in "their" room. Drugs are illegal. And if my child is keeping illegal drugs in his or her room, the fact is that there are illegal drugs in *my* house. I can't plead ignorance to that in a court of law, regardless of how my child feels about his or her privacy.

As with other points we've covered, it's important to be up front about these matters. It's one thing to "sneak" around in your child's room. It's another to be up front with them so they know that you reserve the right to be in their room when you think it's appropriate. You'll work at not abusing that parental right, but you don't want to abdicate your responsibility either. Let your child know where he or she stands on this, and clue them in on the rationale of your rules, values, and principles.

Q: What if I don't' agree with my spouse's view of how to discipline or punish our children?

A: That's more of an issue about your relationship with your spouse than it is about the children. But first, remember that healthy parenting is more about providing appropriate *discipline* for our children than it is about *punishing* our children. There's a real difference. Second, parents have a lot of homework to do before they begin parenting children. Having some honest conversations about family values, family practices, and approaches to discipline is critical. If you don't agree on each other's approaches to parenting and discipline, find a suitable compromise. Remember that most of us learned our parenting skills from our parents. Our preferences often have more to do with the experiences that shaped us—for better or for worse—that with what may be best for us and our children. Work at finding what's "right" for *your* family rather than with what was right or felt comfortable in your family of origin.

Bibliography

Canter, Lee. *Assertive Discipline for Parents.* Harper & Row, Publishers, 1985.

Coles, Robert. *The Spiritual Life of Children.* Houghton Mifflin, 1990.

Friedman, Edwin. *Generation to Generation.* Gilford Press, 1985.

Galindo, Israel. *A Christian Educator's Book of Lists.* Smyth & Helwys Publishers, 2003.

Galindo, Israel. *The Craft of Christian Teaching.* Judson Press, 1998.

Galindo, Israel. *The Bible, Live! Experience-centered Learning Activities for Children.* Judson Press, 1999.

Galindo. Israel. *Let Us Pray: Contemporary Prayers for the Seasons of the Church.* Judson Press, 1999.

Galindo, Israel. *The Tree of All Hearts: Modern Parables for Teaching Faith.* Smyth & Helwys, 2000.

Gilbert, Roberta. *Connecting With Our Children.* John Wiley & Sons, 1999.

Gilbert, Roberta. *Extraordinary Relations.* John Wiley & Sons, 1992.

Ginott, Haim. *Between Parent & Child.* Avon Publishers, 1967.

Ginott, Haim. *Between Parent & Teenager.* Avon Publishers, 1969.

Gottman, John. *The Heart of Parenting: Raising an Emotionally Intelligent Child.* Simon & Schuster, 1997.

Kilpatrick, William. *Why Johnny Can't Tell Right From Wrong.* Simon & Schuster, 1992.

Rekers, George (ed.), *Family Building: Six Qualities of a Strong Family.* Regal Books, 1985.

Richardson, Ron. *Family Ties That Bind.* Self Counsel Press, 1999.

Silverman, Marvin and Lustig, David. *Parent Survival Training: A Complete Guide to Modern Parenting.* Wilshire Book Co., 1978.

ORDER FORM

To order additional copies of *10 Best Parenting Ways to Ruin Your Child,* or other books by Israel Galindo, complete and mail the form below or submit your order by e-mail to: **igalindo@aol.com**

SHIP TO:
Name: _____

Address: _____

City, State, Zip code: _____

Day phone (___) _____

_____ copies of	*10 Best Parenting Ways to Ruin Your Teenager*	@ $12.00 each:	$_____
_____ copies of	*10 Best Parenting Ways to Ruin Your Child*	@ $9.95 each:	$_____
_____ copies of	*The Craft of Christian Teaching*	@ $16.00 each:	$_____
_____ copies of	*The Tree of All Hearts*	@ $15.00 each:	$_____
_____ copies of	*Prayers for the Church*	@ $5.00 each:	$_____
_____ copies of	*Let us Pray*	@ $13.00 each:	$_____
_____ copies of	*Myths: Fact & Fiction about Teaching & Learning*	@ $13.00 each:	$_____
_____ copies of	*The Bible, Live!*	@ $12.00 each:	$_____

Postage and handling @ $1.50 per book: $_____

Virginia residents add 5% sales tax: $_____

TOTAL amount enclosed: $_____

Make check payable to:
Israel Galindo
11904 Rutgers Drive
Richmond, VA 23233